CO[illegible]ISH C[illegible]TIES

A collection of oddities, frivolities & downright stupidities

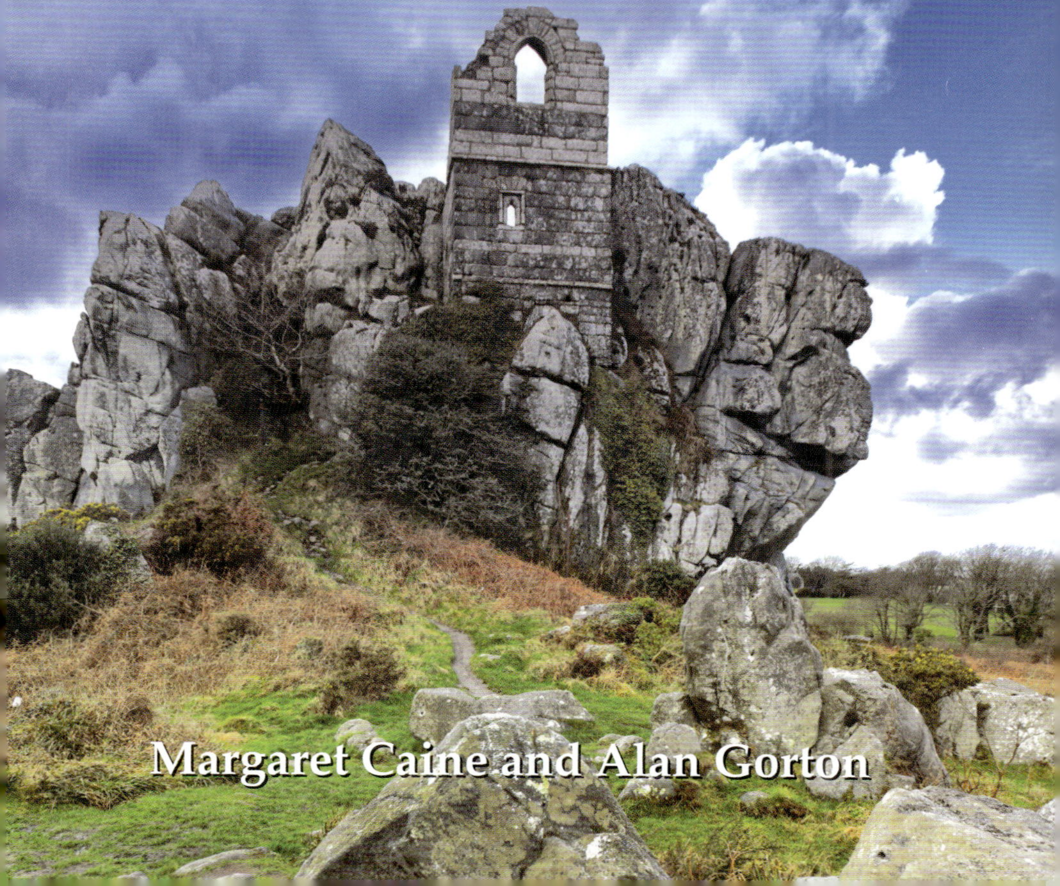

Margaret Caine and Alan Gorton

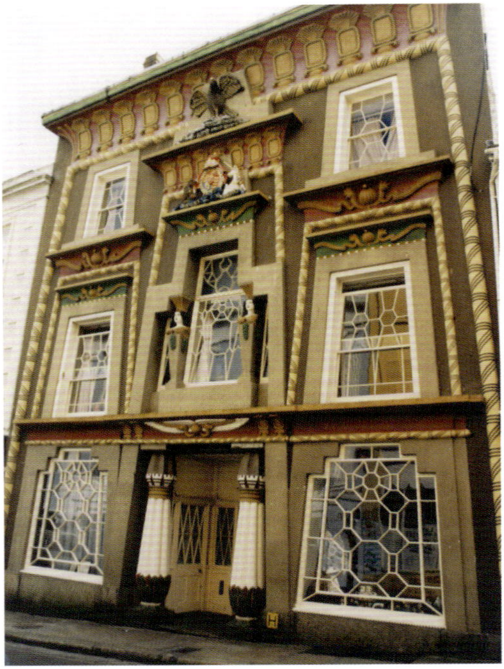

Published by Tor Mark, United Downs Ind Est, St Day, Redruth, Cornwall TR16 5HY www.tormark.co.uk

First published 2013

ISBN 978 085025 432 7

Designed by Alix Wood www.alixwood.co.uk

Picture credits: Cover © Tor Mark: title page © Shutterstock

All other pictures © Margaret Caine

Printed by R Booth Ltd, The Praze, Penryn, Cornwall TR10 8AA

PENTILLIE – tomb with a view

Location:
off A388, three miles north of Saltash

OS map:
201 41016521

Sat nav:
PL12 6QD

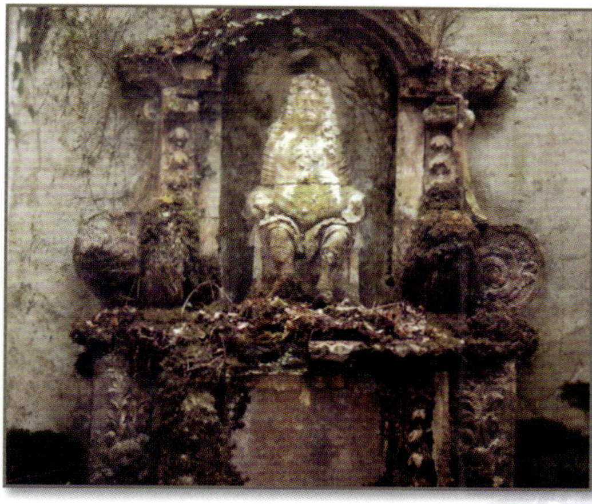

How a man of humble origins could become a titled and wealthy landowner is still shrouded in controversy, but James Tillie did just that. He became the Coryton family agent for their large estate in the Tamar valley. In 1692, at the early age of 42, Sir John Coryton suffered a mysteriously sudden, agonising death. After a two-year gap, James Tillie married his widow and so acquired the estate. Rumours were rife but allegations that Tillie had poisoned his employer were never proven.

First, the now Sir James Tillie commissioned the building of Pentillie. Next, he built a three-storey mausoleum for himself on his estate, called Mount Ararat. He died on November 15, 1713, and in his will ordered that his body must be placed inside, fastened into a throne-like chair, dressed in his finest clothes, wig, hat and rings, together with a chest of his personal possessions.

There he intended to sit and await resurrection, which he thought would be within two years. Two years passed, his body and the roof of the mausoleum deteriorated, and his remains were decently buried. A life-sized statue was placed on the seat.

NB: *the mausoleum can only be reached with permission from the estate.*

MOUNT EDGCUMBE – a folly...

Location:
off B3247, five miles south of Saltash

OS map:
folly 201 4568 5261
obelisk 201 4614 5339

Sat nav:
PL10 1HZ

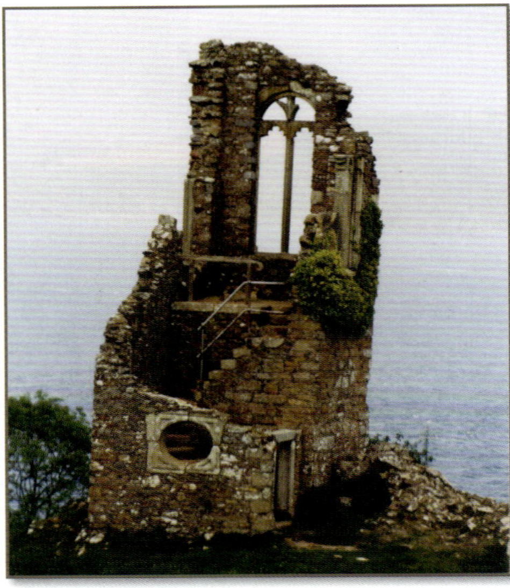

In the 18th century, there was a fashionable interest in classical and romantic ruins – satirised by Jane Austen in *Northanger Abbey* – with estate owners adorning their parks with new 'ruins', temples, statues, pagodas and similar exotica to give them the fashionable 'classical' appearance, to provide points of interest, vistas and focal points for walks and summer picnic parties.

Successive Earls of Mount Edgcumbe scattered a number of such buildings around the 800 acres of their parkland – a small Tuscan temple called Thomson's Seat, Milton's Temple, the Arch, the Red Seat, and a folly, called simply the Ruin, a crumbling ecclesiastical-looking artificial 'ruined' castle constructed in that 'genuine' state in 1747! It was located specially to take advantage of the spectacular views overlooking Drake's Island in Plymouth Sound, with different perspectives from the ground, the flight of steps and the large arched, traceried window.

... and a pig

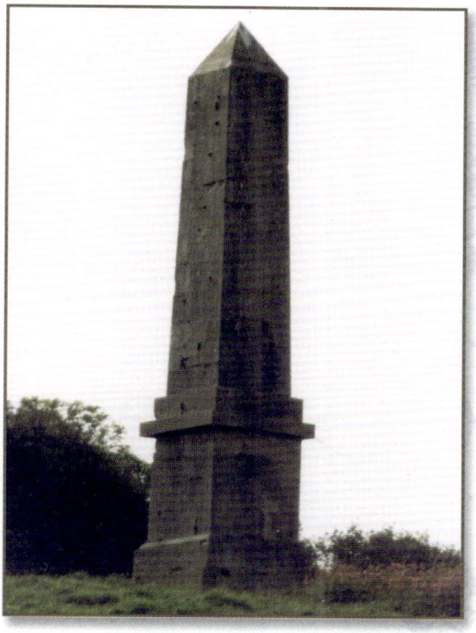

One eccentric Countess of Mount Edgcumbe was so devoted to her pet pig, Cupid, that it became her constant companion. Cupid went everywhere with her, to house parties, on visits to London, and lived out his days in considerable comfort. When he died, the Countess was so distraught that she had a massive obelisk, thirty feet tall (9m), erected over his grave in the grounds of the estate. A report in a local paper claimed that Cupid was buried in a gold casket, the spot being marked by the obelisk on the instruction of the Countess. The bizarre relationship and the lady's grief became the subject of an ode by the satirist Dr. John Wolcot, under his pseudonym Peter Pindar:

Ode To The Countess Of Mount Edgcumbe
On The Death Of Her Pet Pig Cupid

Oh! Dry those tears so round and big,
Nor waste in sighs your precious wind
Death only takes a little pig.
Your Lord and son are still behind!

The obelisk was moved in the 1860s to a hill near Cremyll, outside the estate. Was this to give it greater prominence, or to get at the gold casket in which Cupid was allegedly buried? We will never know.

POLPERRO – two interesting houses

Location:
on A387, five miles east of Fowey

OS map:
201 2087 5081

Sat nav:
PL13 2RD

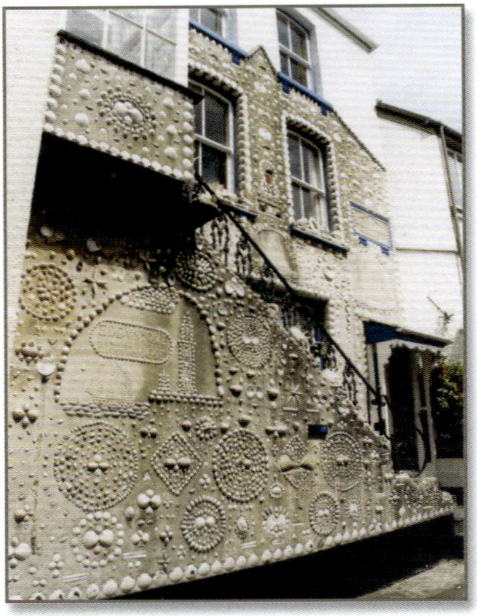

Though it's Polperro now, over the centuries it's been Porpira (possibly meaning 'Pyra's cove' when it was recorded in 1379), Porthpera, Porthpire, Porth Pyre and Polparrow – though just why a Porth (a 'cove') became a Pol (a 'pool') is puzzling. Fortunately, what we come to see is still enchanting: sheltered in its narrow, wooded ravine, a jumble of cottages tumbles to the sea, each one different but making a pleasing whole.

As you wander through the village, look carefully at these houses. The House on Props may appear picturesque beside a stream but was built on supports for a very practical reason – to keep it safely above the flood level. Tucked away in The Warren, the whimsical Shell House was a fisherman's cottage, until it was bought by Samuel Puckey when he retired from the Navy. Beginning in 1937, patiently over the next 5 years he encrusted it with shells he had spent a lifetime collecting from all over the world, decorating his house with intricate patterns, scallops around the windows, pictures of ships, the Eddystone Lighthouse, towers, circles, stars, diamonds, squares, butterflies and flowers.

FOWEY – dues payable

Location:
on A3082, six miles east of St. Austell

OS map:
200 1429 5162

Sat nav:
PL23 1NH

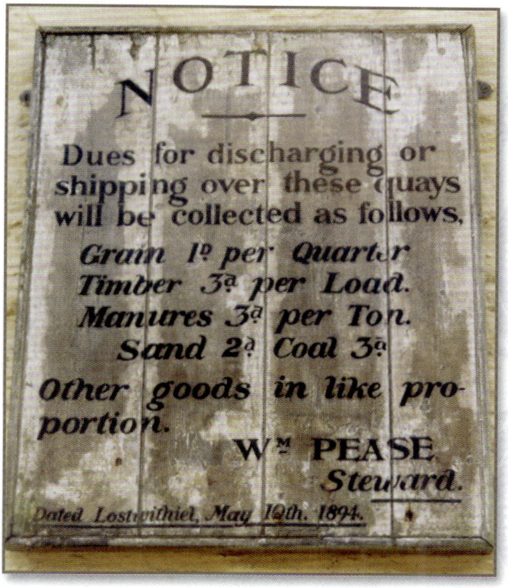

Fowey is rightly proud of its many literary associations, as the setting for Sir Arthur Quiller-Couch (Q)'s novel *Troy Town* and the "little grey sea town" described by Sea Rat in Kenneth Grahame's *The Wind in the Willows*. Here too, Daphne du Maurier began her first novel *The Loving Spirit*.

But this superb natural harbour has long been a working port, which extended far up the river. Pont Pill Creek is now a quiet backwater giving the impression it is miles from anywhere. It was not always so. Less than a century ago boats came regularly to collect cargoes of grain, timber, coal and sand. The shipping dues payable in 1894 are posted on the farmhouse wall.

MENABILLY – a medieval romance

Location:
one mile north of
Fowey on the A3082

OS map:
200 1139 5237

Sat nav:
PL24 2TN

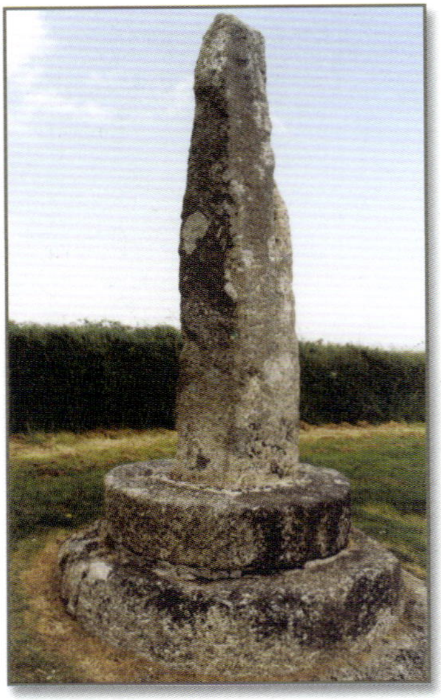

Just before you drop steeply into Fowey, by the roadside is a solitary seven-foot tall (2.12m) monolith with a Latin inscription, 'Drustanus Fili Cunomorus' (Here lies Tristan, son of Cynfawr).

Sir Tristan is one knight in the Arthurian legends who may have been based on a real person. In one of the most popular romantic poems of the Middle Ages, Tristan, the son of King Mark of Cornwall, falls in love with his father's new wife, Queen Iseult, only for it all to end tragically. This stone has the Latin version of his name, Drustanus. Cunomorus was recorded in the Dark Ages as Cynfawr, who ruled the Celtic kingdom of Dumnonia, then later as King Mark. So both Tristan (Drustanus) and King Mark (Cunomorus) did exist, though their link to King Arthur is only tenuous.

Moreover, the stone stood originally just south of Castle Dore, the Iron Age earthwork which King Mark used, two miles away along the B3269. It was moved to its present location when new roads were being built so it doesn't now mark Tristan's grave.

LOSTWITHIEL – the longest lease

Location:
on A390, six miles south-east of Bodmin

OS map:
200 1038 5983

Sat nav:
PL22 0EG

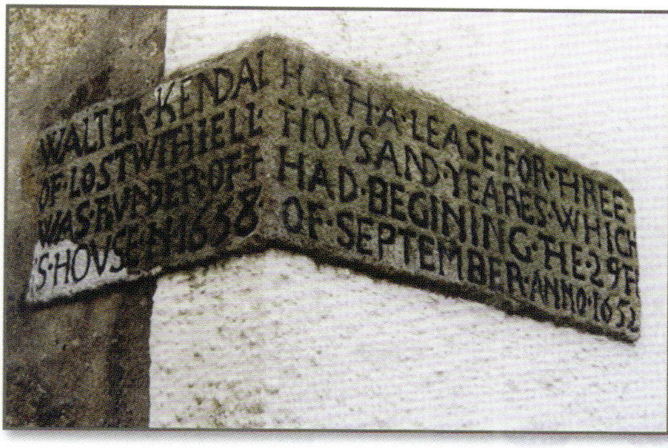

The Kendals of Pelyn have a long association with Lostwithiel, representing the Borough as MPs from as long ago as 1365 and serving the town as Mayors and Recorders and the county as Magistrates and High Sheriffs. They were not above using their influence to their own advantage. In one instance, Walter, Richard and Thomas Kendal "unlawfully did make profits for themselves from Corporation property" until in 1603 the Mayor and Corporation filed a complaint in the Chancery Court against those "... who did keep and withhold from the said town the market place ..." – and won.

By that time, Walter Kendal owned a number of properties, including the town mill. Quite obviously he was a keen negotiator and by having details of a lease inscribed on a corner-stone of the old Malthouse made sure everyone knew about it! Especially as the lease would not expire until 4652! This most curious legal document in Cornwall reads:

WALTER KENDAL OF LOSTWITHIEL WAS FoVNDER OFF'S HOUSE 1658: HATH A LEASE FOR THREE THOUSAND YEARES WHICH HAD BEGINING THE 29 OF SEPTEMBER ANNO 1652

ROCHE – St. Michael's Chapel

Location:
on B3274, five miles north of St. Austell

OS map:
200 5964 9913

Sat nav:
PL26 8EN

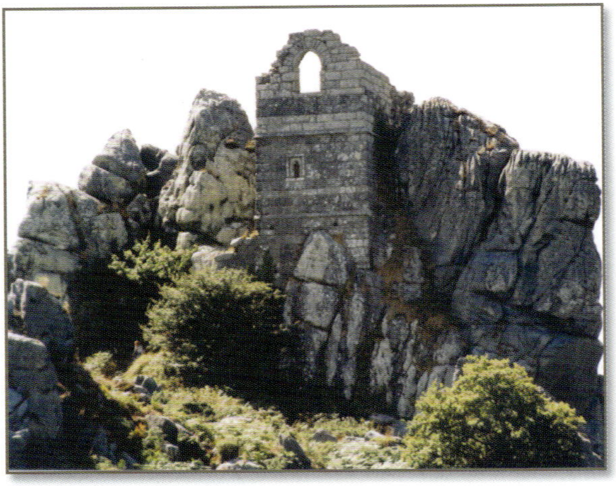

As you drive through Roche, you pass a huge quartz outcrop glowering starkly down on the Cornish countryside. In the early years of Christianity, a hermit, probably St. Gonand who suffered from leprosy, hacked a cell into these rocks. In 1409 a tiny chapel was built above it, not by carving the rock face but by cutting chunks out and somehow carrying them up to the top.

Predictably, stories have become associated with both the hermit's cell and chapel. The earliest tells of the last male heir of Tregarrick who also contracted leprosy and moved into the cell to avoid spreading the disease. His daughter, Gundred, continued to bring him food and water, a devotion which led to her sainthood and the village church dedicated to her.

Another concerns that favourite Cornish bogeyman Jan Tregeagle who climbed Roche Rocks to gain sanctuary in the chapel. However, only his head would fit through the window: his body remained outside, exposed to the snarling fangs of the hounds of hell that were chasing him. Eventually a priest came to his rescue and sent him back to his endless task of emptying Dozmary Pool with a limpet shell.

VERYAN – unique houses

Location:
off A3078, seven miles south-east of Truro

OS map:
204 9165 3962

Sat nav:
TR2 5RL

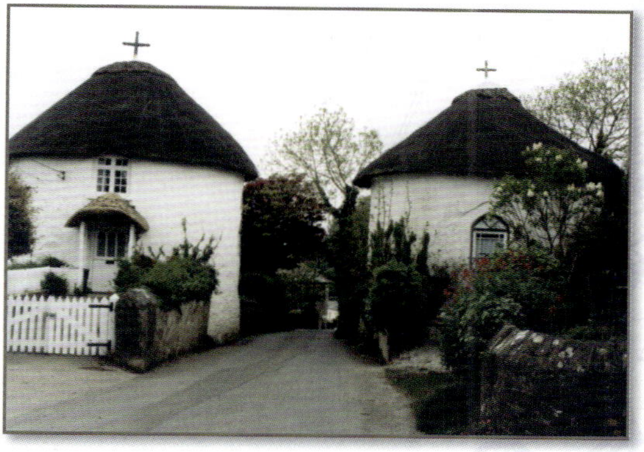

Veryan boasts five thatched 'round houses'. They were built for £50 each by Hugh Rowe of Lostwithiel for Revd. Jeremiah Trist, who was both squire and vicar at the beginning of the nineteenth century.

Those were days of superstition. Some people claim he built them for his daughters and made them round so that the Devil would have no north side to enter by and no dark corners in which to hide. The crosses surmounting the top added another line of defence. There is a pair at what was either end of the village with a fifth in the centre so that if the Evil One did come prowling he wouldn't be able to enter the village and would leave Veryan in peace.

It is interesting to note though that *Worgan's Agricultural Survey* of 1811 published almost identical designs, and these were intended as labourers' cottages.

FALMOUTH – a pyramid in Cornwall...

Location:
on A39, nine miles south of Truro

OS map:
pyramid 204 8126 3234
pipe 204 8150 3240

Sat nav: TR11 3JT

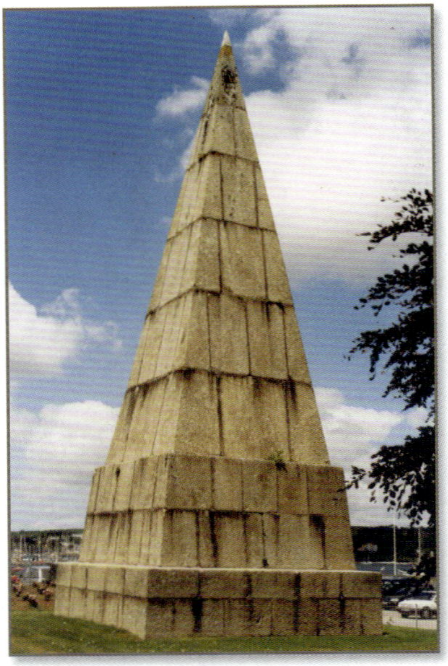

Phoenicians and Romans came in search of tin to what we now know as Falmouth, but it remained a tiny fishing settlement called Smithwick until in the late sixteenth century. Its development was orchestrated by the Killigrew family. They were an enterprising and often outrageous lot. Some engaged in piracy, some were knighted, some were debtors and one built Cornwall's first lighthouse at the Lizard.

It seemed the family line was about to end when Sir Peter Killigrew died in 1704, after the death in infancy of one heir and the loss of another, George, who was killed in a duel. Then Martin Lister married Anne Killigrew and adopted the family name. Instead of producing an heir, he erected in 1737–38 a granite pyramidal monument opposite Arwenack House, where it would remain "a beauty to the Harbour without limitation of time". Inside, about half way up, is a sealed bottle containing historic information put there by a later bailiff of the manor; higher still is another bottle, surreptitiously placed there by the workmen.

...and the King's pipe

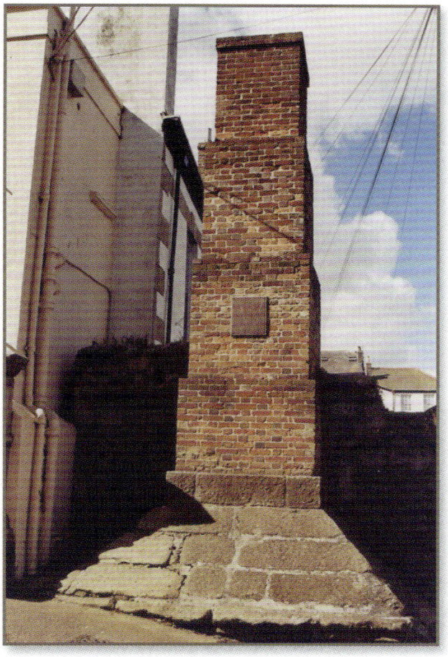

'Free-trading', as the Cornish euphemistically called smuggling, was an important part of the local economy and people from all walks of life – including the Killigrews – joined in. Falmouth was one of its centres and in the 18th century a four-tiered, brick-built furnace on Custom House Quay (another Killigrew construction), was built so excisemen could burn the cargoes of contraband tobacco they had seized. Not surprisingly, it was nick-named 'the King's Pipe'.

Its main function was symbolic. Though apparently hidden from the town, it was highly visible to seafarers as they came into harbour. But only damaged tobacco was burnt: the majority was auctioned off to augment the Revenue's exchequer.

MANACCAN – a unique fig tree

Location:
seven miles east of Helston

OS map:
204 7648 2500

Sat nav:
TR12 6HN

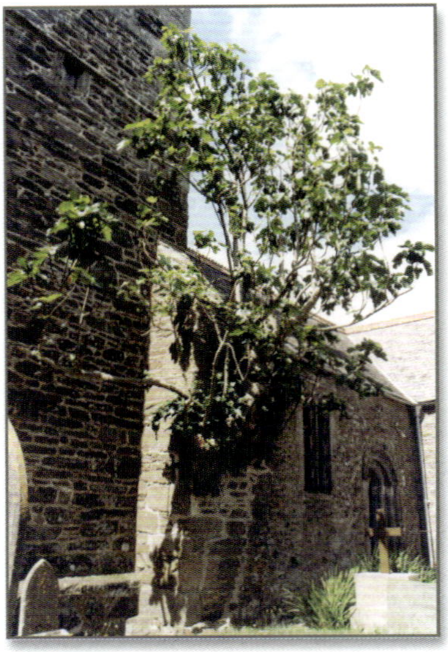

Perched saucily on a hillside, Manaccan is a delight. The church's dedication to St. Manacca is almost certainly an invention. In Cornish, 'managh' means 'monk' and 'an' means 'the', so Manaccan is simply 'the monk'.

A record of 1893 described "on the south side of the tower is a large fig tree, growing out of the church wall", more than a century old, with a trunk eighteen inches (half a metre) in diameter; its roots penetrate the thickness of the wall.

It is still here. So who planted it? Why? Now more than two centuries old, taking full advantage of the Cornish sun, it has flourished in a symbiotic relationship with the church, rooting in the rubble infill of the solid Norman walls and penetrating beneath the benches inside. But be careful: ill luck befalls anyone who picks figs from this tree.

POLDHU – secret messages

Location:
off B3296, six miles south of Helston

OS map:
203 6637 1941

Sat nav:
TR12 7HB

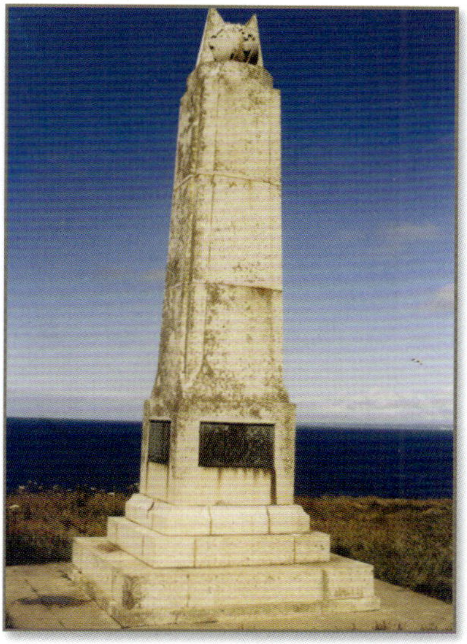

On the windswept summit of the cliffs is an imposing granite column. It is the only reminder of the momentous events that took place here.

Guglielmo Marconi came to England in 1896 and with Sir William Preece, Chief Engineer at the Post Office, looked for a suitable site to establish a research station for sending telegraphy signals. They chose Poldhu. But on the other side of Mount's Bay, at Porthcurno, the Eastern Telegraph Company had been set up in 1872 with a monopoly on world communications by laying ocean cables. Marconi was seen as a threat.

By 1900, Marconi's new structure dominated the landscape, four large, spidery towers, a sea of steel masts and a maze of wiring overhead. On 12 December 1901, signals from here were received by Marconi at St. John's, Newfoundland: three faint dots, Morse code for the letter 'S'. This toe of Cornwall was now the centre for long distance communications, but still the two companies couldn't work in harmony and kept a close eye (and ear) on each other's activities.

SANCREED – what is a fogou?

Location:
five miles south-west of Penzance

OS map:
203 4025 2882

Sat nav:
TR20 8RB

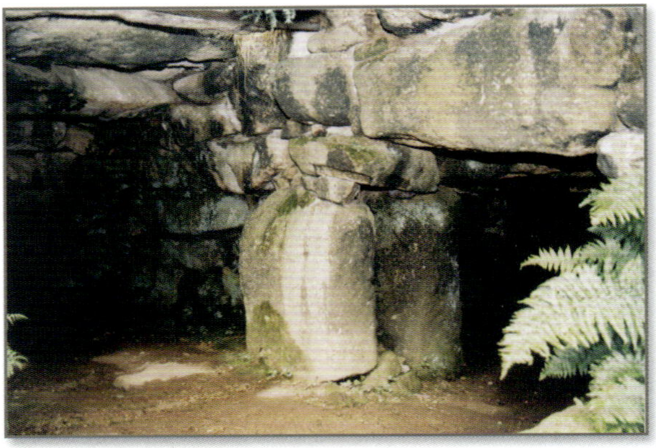

In the middle of the Iron Age village at Carn Euny is an outstanding example of a fogou (from the local word for 'cave'), 66ft (20.1m) long, partly underground, covered with earth and stones, lined and roofed with enormous granite slabs. It is deep enough to stand upright inside and has a circular chamber leading off it – though why, no-one knows.

Fogous were built from around 500BC to AD 400, spanning the late Iron Age to the Roman period, but why did these villagers go to such trouble to make one? The time and effort must have been enormous. Were they hiding places in times of danger? Or caches where smelted tin was concealed? Could they have been a place for mystical, pre-Christian rituals or astronomical calculators, standing at focal points of both cosmic and terrestrial energies broadcast through the ley lines system?

No-one is certain. Current thinking is more prosaic, that they were Iron Age larders, cool, underground chambers where meat, grain and birds' eggs could be preserved for a lean season.

BREAGE – take warning!

Location:
on A394, five miles west of Helston

OS map:
203 6174 2849

Sat nav:
TR13 9PD

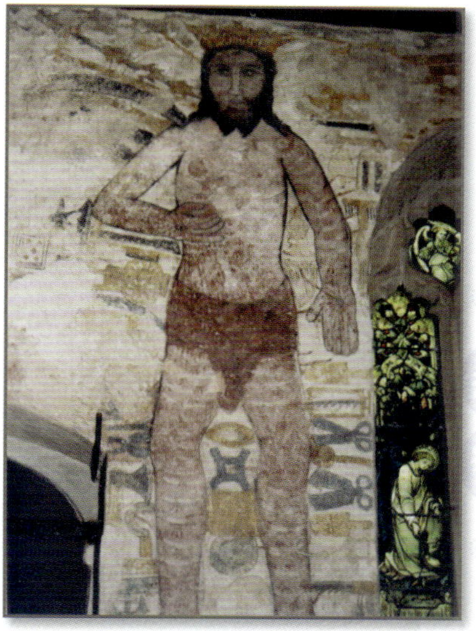

St. Breaca's church is home to a wonderful collection of nine late-15th-century wall paintings, created by monks who travelled the country decorating churches. However, on 23 April, 1549, three commissioners, appointed to ensure that religious changes were carried out, visited Breage and ordered the destruction of the windows, rood screen and loft, and the walls to be whitewashed. As a result, the murals lay hidden for 350 years.

One dating from c.1470 is surely the strangest you will ever see. A massive, crowned figure of Christ stares at everyone who comes into the church. Dressed only in loin-cloth, he is covered with profusely bleeding wounds, surrounded by shears, knives, fish-hooks, hammers and tongs, even a cart and some dice. What does this mean? The mural is a symbolic warning against working on a Sunday, which should be set aside as holy.

ST. LEVAN – a prophetic stone

Location:
three miles south-east of Land's End

OS map:
203 3805 2233

Sat nav:
TR19 6JT

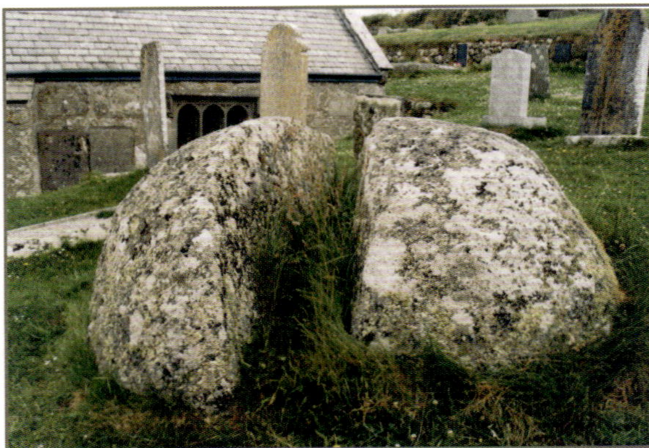

Ancient rocks and boulders seem to attract weird tales, most of them involving the Devil's habit of hurling them around, though happily he always seemed to miss his target. This one is different. Levan, a holy man in the 6th or 7th century, lived on a diet of one fresh fish a day. Between fishing trips he used to rest on an enormous boulder near the church porch. One day, when he was old, he struck the stone with his fist, and split it in two. He then prophesied the end of the world:

When with panniers astride, A pack-horse one can ride
Through St. Levan's Stone, The world will be done.

Fortunately, the gap in the boulder is only between 14 and 20 inches (35-50cm) wide, far too narrow for a packhorse even without panniers. Robert Hunt wrote in 1841:

> *It is more than fifty years since I first made the acquaintance, as a child, with the St. Levan Stone and it may be a satisfaction to many to know that the progress of separation is an extremely slow one... the pack-horse and panniers will not be able to pass through the rock for many thousands of years to come.*

We can rest easy.

NEWLYN – *Mystery*'s epic adventure

Location:
on B3315, two miles south of Penzance

OS map:
203 4627 2904

Sat nav:
TR18 5QZ

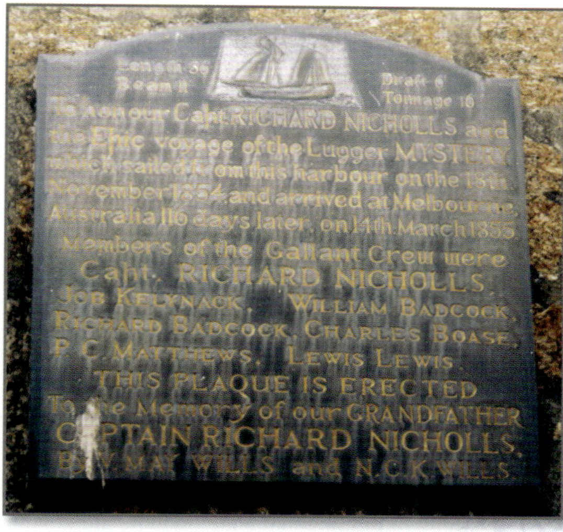

A plaque outside the Mission to Deep Sea Fishermen in Newlyn depicts a small lugger in full sail. Why? The story began when a local man, Charles Kelynack, emigrated to Australia to prospect for gold. The crew of the *Mystery* were eager to join him, selling their boat to raise the passage money. However, after a few pints in a Penzance inn they talked instead of sailing there. Even when sober, they wouldn't change their minds.

The seven men adapted the 36ft (11m) *Mystery*, then loaded it with fresh water and provisions, including salt meat and hard tack. On 18 November, 1854, cheered by crowds on the shore, they set sail with only a compass, sextant and barometer for navigation. During the epic voyage they experienced everything the sea could throw at them. It was four months before their families heard of their safe arrival in Melbourne on 14 March, 1855, after 116 days, a feat of seamanship unparalleled at that time.

And what about striking gold? In all the excitement they seemed to have forgotten about that and after a while most of them returned to Newlyn.

PENZANCE – an unusual house...

Location:
6/7 Chapel Street
Penzance

OS map:
house 203 4672 3035
tree 203 4683 3081

Sat nav:
house TR18 4AW
tree TR18 2PL

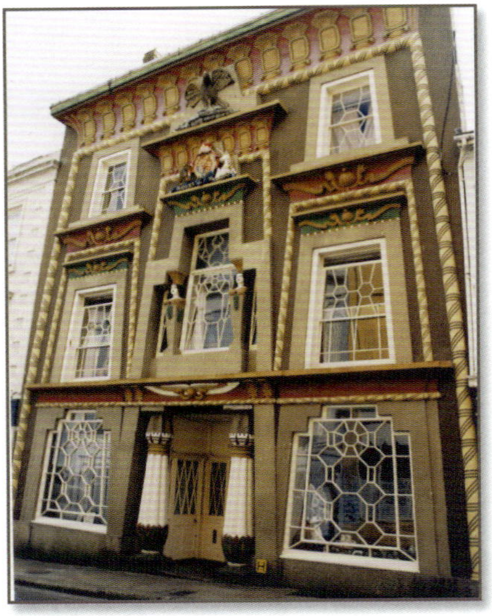

One of the most unusual and colourful house facades in the whole of Great Britain is in Chapel Street. Its flamboyance is accentuated by ornate lotus columns, stylised cornices, and sphinx-like decoration.

It was designed in 1835 by John Foulston of Plymouth, in a style that was briefly fashionable after Napoleon's 1798 campaign in Egypt. It may be a copy of Egyptian Hall built in Piccadilly, London, in 1812, but the architect was inspired by the Temple of Hat-hor at Dendra in Egypt.

The original owner was John Lavin, a local mineralogist. He lived here and housed his extensive geological collection in his shop on the ground floor. But the collection was sold by Lavin's son and became part of Oxford University Museum. By the end of the 1960s the building had fallen into disrepair but in 1973 was restored to its original splendour.

Now you can rent part of it for your holiday or just stand and wonder at the ornate designs – and calculate how long it must take to re-paint it!

...and modern street art

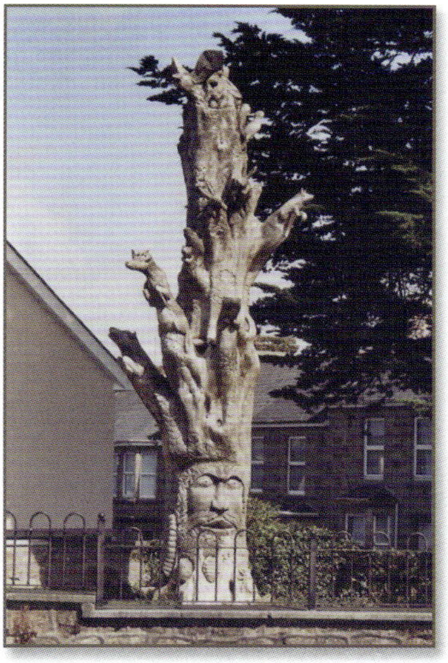

During the Victorian era, Monterey Cypress (*Cupressus Macracarpa*) trees were planted throughout the southern part of Cornwall, where they thrived. Most lived for about 100 years until they became dangerous and had to be felled.

This one in St. Clare Street, Penzance, was spared. But what to do with it? It was decided by the then current owners of the land, Penwith Housing Association and Penzance Town Council, to commission a carving, so Cornwall-based sculptor Peter Martin was appointed and from September 2009 spent weeks up the 30ft tree (9m), watched by fascinated passers-by, as he transformed the dead trunk, creating a Green Man theme with woodland animals and flowers. It has become a welcome addition to local landmarks, which residents admire and visitors find fascinating.

If you are interested, in 2011 the same sculptor carved a Monterey Cypress trunk which had split at Wyevale Lelant Garden Centre in Hayle, and Craig Harris has produced 8 carvings spread around the lake at Tehidy Woods and two 8ft (2.5m) totem poles in St. Buryan.

PAUL – the last to speak only Cornish?

Location:
two miles south of Newlyn

OS map:
203 4650 2718

Sat nav:
TR19 6UA

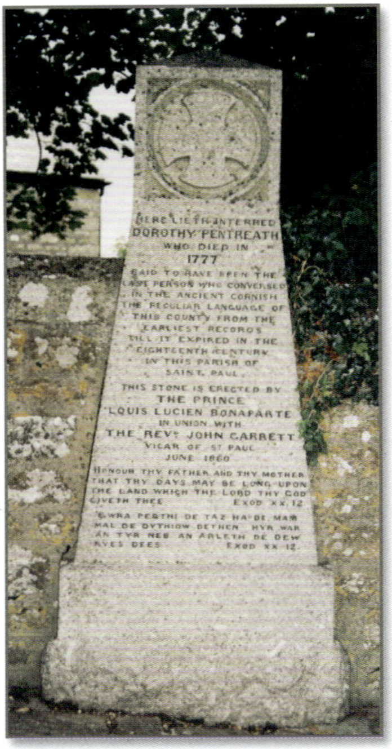

Paul churchyard has an unusual monument set into the wall. It is dedicated to Dolly Pentreath who was buried in 1777 under her married name of Jefferey. According to many folk, she was the last person who spoke only Cornish but William Bodenor, who was also buried here, is also cited as a later speaker of only Cornish, while John Davey (1812–92) of Boswenack's memorial in Zennor claims this distinction. There is though some acceptance that the last monoglot speaker of Cornish was Chesten Marchant, who died in 1676 at Gwythian.

Dolly appears to have gained her reputation by jabbering some words of Cornish to impress visitors if the price was right – but cursed them for free if she wasn't paid. How the stone came to be erected here is as unusual as she was. Being near fashionable Penzance, aristocratic visitors often meandered this way. One was Prince Louis Lucien Bonaparte, an antiquarian and linguist who, intrigued by the stories he had heard about her, decided with the vicar, Revd. John Garbett, to honour her with a lengthy (and partially irrelevant) inscription, part of which is written in Cornish, and that she was reputed to be 102 when she died.

TREEN – the Logan rock

Location:
four miles south-east of Land's End

OS map:
203 3969 2202

Sat nav:
TR19 6LG

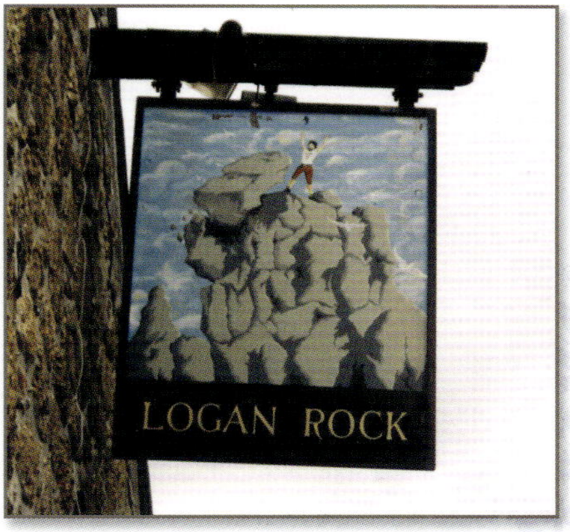

Among the jagged crags and large tumbled boulders of Treryn Dinas is the Logan Rock, a huge stone weighing sixty-six tons that at one time was so finely balanced it would 'log' or sway when pushed.

That is until 1824 when Lieutenant Goldsmith of the Royal Navy, nephew of the poet Oliver Goldsmith, together with a group of fellow-sailors from the Revenue cutter *Nimble*, dislodged it and pushed it over the edge. Such was the public outcry that the Admiralty ordered him, under threat of removing his commission, to reinstate the stone to its original place at his own expense. Young Goldsmith had to hire men to erect a complex system of derricks and hoists at a cost of £130. 8s. 6d, which almost bankrupted him, and included an item

To Mr William Charnalls for sixty St. Just men who did nothing but drink beer to the value of 13s.6d.

The stone never rocked as before and Treen lost so much of its trade from the visitors who wanted to see this natural wonder that it became known as 'Goldsmith's deserted village'. Fortunately, the arrival in Penzance of the Great Western Railway helped to restore some of its popularity.

BOTALLACK – a mine beneath the sea

Location:
west of B3306, two miles north of St. Just

OS map:
203 3628 3385

Sat nav:
TR19 7QQ

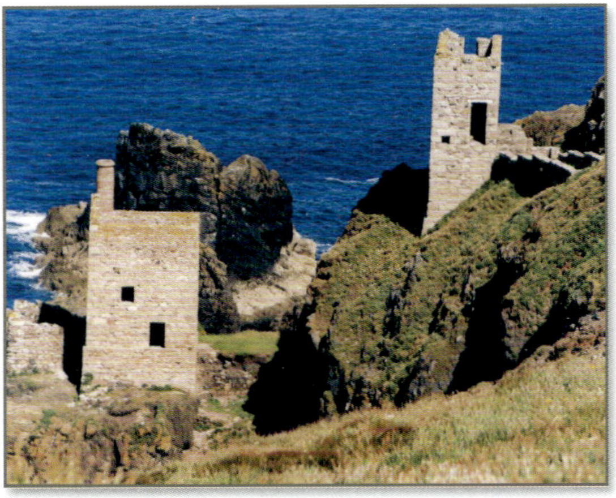

The Cornish landscape is haunted by silhouettes of chimneys and engine houses. Botallack's former engine houses perch dramatically above the Atlantic. In their time the maze of platforms, ladders and machinery descending the cliffs was a source of wonder. Tunnels 7ft by 4ft (2 x 1m) were cut into a rich mineralised lode, worked at a depth of 350 fathoms below sea level and extending for a mile under the sea bed itself.

J. A. Paris, writing in 1824, was sympathetic

> *... in these caverns of darkness are many human beings, for a small precarious pittance, constantly digging for ore, regardless of the horrors which surround them, and the roar of the Atlantic ocean incessantly rolling over their heads. We should feel pity for the wretch who, as an atonement for his crimes, should be compelled to undergo the tasks which the Cornish miner voluntarily undertakes and as cheerfully performs.*

In its heyday, the mine employed 500 men, women and children. Now only ruins remain, picturesque but gently decaying.

PORTH NANVEN – fascinating geology

Location:
half a mile from
St. Just

OS map:
203 3559 2989

Sat nav:
TR19 7NP

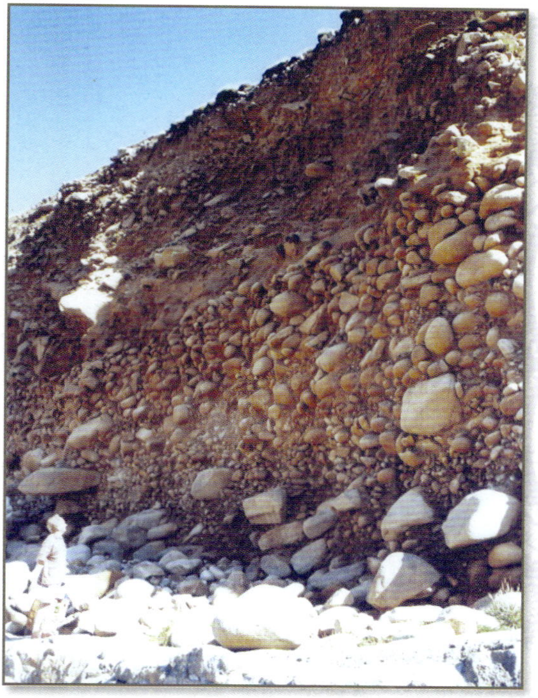

You will have to search for this cove in Cot Valley. Sometimes referred to as 'Dinosaur Egg Beach' or 'Fossil Beach', it has a remarkable collection of boulders. They come in all sizes, from pebbles like hens' eggs to others a metre or more in length – all ovoid. You would be correct in assuming they were shaped by the sea, but it was 120,000 years ago during a warm inter-glacial period.

Then ice caps in northern Britain melted, the beach tilted upwards and, if you stand on the beach and look back you will see a wall of rounded rocks – previously on the sea floor – embedded high above your head waiting to break away and join those on the 'modern' beach below: the change in sea level left this ancient beach suspended as the cliff. Above them still, is a thick layer of periglacial head deposits, angular pieces from 100,000 to 20,000 years ago, showing that it has been very cold here in not so distant times.

ZENNOR – true love

Location:
B3306, five miles west of St. Ives

OS map:
203 4550 3850

Sat nav:
TR26 3BV

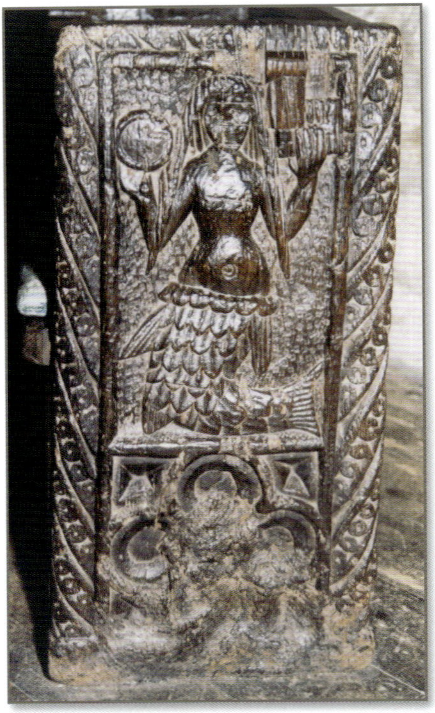

Isolated from other communities by land and unnoticed from the sea, like most medieval Christians the folk of Zennor believed in mermaids, as warnings of the snares which await them in the wickedness of the world. Or they could be about a love story.

No mermaid is more magical than this lascivious portrait, holding a mirror and a comb, carved on a bench end in the church. She was attracted from her watery habitat by the singing of a chorister, Matthew Trewella, and would sit, listening, in a long dress at the back of the church. He in turn was captivated by her beauty. One evening, she lured him away to join her beneath the waves, where they lived on the sea-bed in Pendour Cove. The boy's father tried to get his son to come home by paying the village wood-carver to create this portrayal of sensuous charm to tempt her out of the sea and the boy to return home – but the ruse failed. Matthew Trewella was never seen again. Though, if you listen carefully on a summer's evening you can hear the pair of lovers singing from the depths below.

GWENNAP PIT – John Wesley

Location:
one mile south of Redruth

OS map:
203 7176 4168

Sat nav:
TR16 5HH

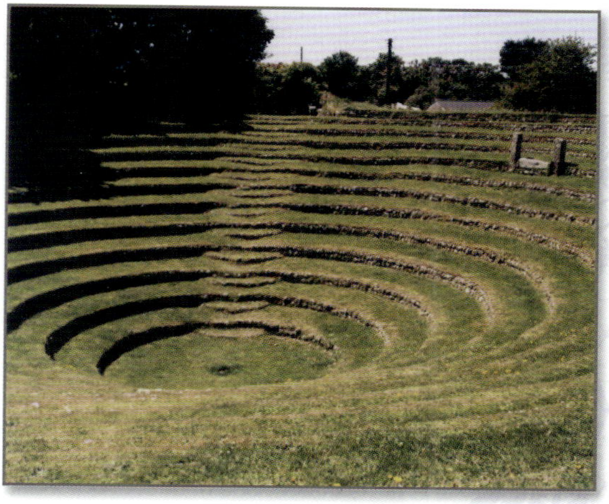

Gwennap was once the centre of the world's greatest copper and tin producing region. The men who worked the mines often died young, leaving widows with families, while others fell ill, unable to carry on.

John Wesley's message brought hope. He visited Cornwall over thirty times, but his favourite preaching place was at Gwennap Pit. It is thought that the collapse of underground mining excavations created this 'natural' steep-sided amphitheatre, with excellent acoustics, about 100 yards (91.4m) in diameter at the top reducing to about 5 yards (4.6m) at the bottom.

He first came here in 1762, and in 1773 attracted a congregation of 32,000, "the largest assembly I ever preached to!" The pit held a special place in the hearts of the mining community too. In 1806 local miners volunteered to cut the twelve circular terraces for seating. The pit is now part of the Cornish Mining World Heritage Site.

CRANTOCK – in the stocks

Location:
two miles west of
Newquay

OS map:
200 7904 6061

Sat nav:
TR8 5RH

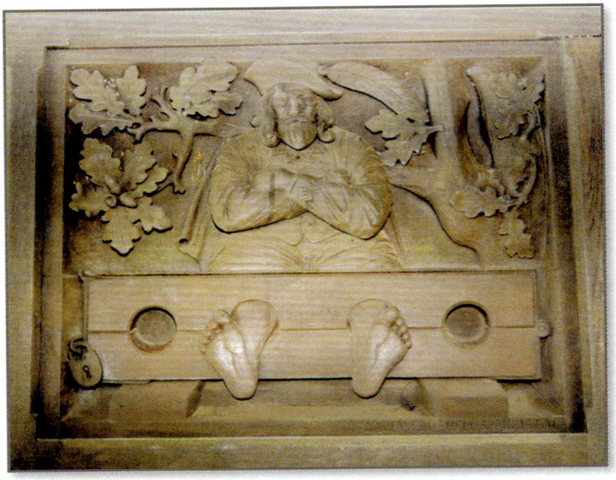

The village stocks outside St. Carantoc's church have a very curious carving of a man with his bare feet fastened in the holes, his arms crossed, a feather in his jaunty hat. It looks like it should be a memorial, but the inscription actually tells a different story:

The last man in Crantock stocks (circa 1817) was William Tinney of west Pentire, a smuggler's son and vagabond. He robbed, with violence, a widow of Cubert parish and was placed, to abide justice, in Crantock stocks then standing in the church tower.

By negligence or design he was insufficiently secured, and shortly afterwards appeared on the top of the tower. He had cut the rope from the tenor bell and by this he lowered himself to the nave roof. Climbing to the eastern gable of the choir and sliding down it, he dropped to the churchyard grass and in the sympathetic view of certain village worthies bolted, got off to sea and was never brought to justice or seen in the neighbourhood again.

Though William Tinney spent only a short time in the stocks, his effigy sits here for eternity.

NEWQUAY – "hevva, hevva!"

Location:
on Towan Head,
Newquay

OS map:
200 8067 6239

Sat nav:
TR7 1EN

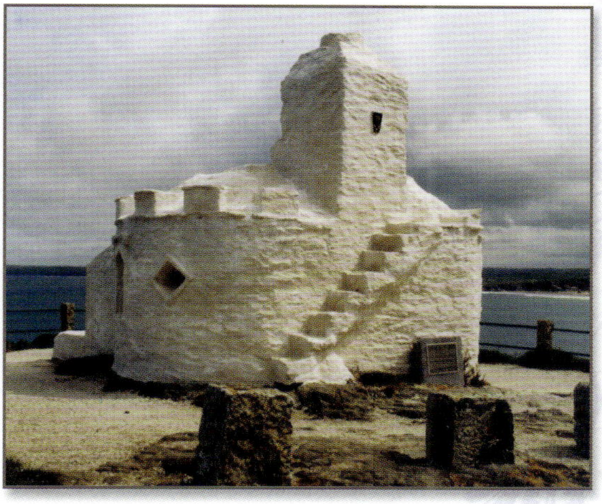

"Hevva, Hevva" was probably the most welcome cry heard in Cornwall in days gone by, for it meant that the look-out man or 'huer' had spotted an approaching shoal of pilchards. Although this cliff-top Huer's House is more like an eccentric folly, it was very much a functional look-out post. When the air resounded to the huer's cries, everyone would rush to man the seine boats, or prepare the 'cellars' for tons of fish to be landed.

The huer directed operations by semaphore with a furze bush or canvas-covered hoops, controlling the movement of boats so they could surround the shoal and simultaneously 'shoot the seine'. His work demanded skill, as an advertisement of 1848 testified.

Wanted, for a Pilchard Sean, at Newquay a steady intelligent man as huer, and an active man, with some decision about him as master seaner. None need apply but those who have had much experience in Pilchard Fishing.

With the decline in the pilchard shoals in the late C19th, the arrival of the railway allowed Newquay to develop a new industry – tourism. The huer's hut stands as a reminder of the great days of seining – the days of 'fish, tin and copper'.

ST. MAWGAN – churchyard regulations

Location:
five miles north-east of Newquay

OS map:
200 8726 6597

Sat nav:
TR8 4ER

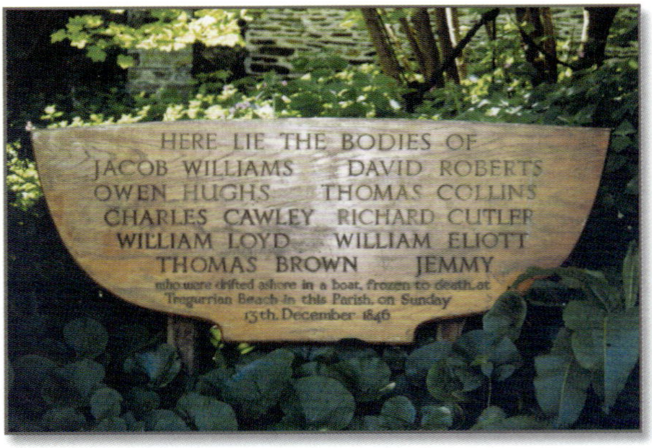

Nowadays, a formidable document, *Churchyard Regulations*, is issued to churchwardens, and Regulation No. 5 gives a list of items prohibited on graves. This would certainly preclude the memorial here, to nine men and a boy found frozen to death in their life-boat which drifted ashore at Beacon Cove in December, 1846, after their ship was wrecked nearby.

It is an historic as well as an unusual headstone because these men were the first to be buried here following the introduction of the Burial of Drowned Persons Act 1808.

This was the work of two Cornish men. John Hearle Tremayne used his maiden speech to Parliament to describe the appalling treatment of drowned bodies. Then, he and Thomas Grylls, an MP and Helston solicitor, by their Act ensured it became compulsory for bodies from shipwrecks to be given Christian burial at public expense, together with rewards for those who discovered them.

The memorial takes the form of the stern of a boat, inscribed with the names of the victims, though one, a boy Jemmy, has no known surname.

ST. COLUMB MINOR – Cornish sports

Location:
on A39, six miles east of Newquay

OS map:
200 9138 6355

Sat nav:
TR9 6AL

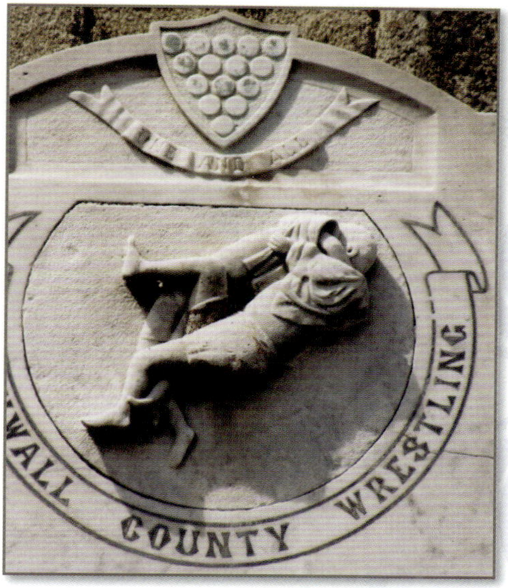

Each Shrove Tuesday, St. Columb Major wakes up to a raucous game of hurling. Play starts when a silver-coated apple wood ball is hurled high above the crowd, and the rest is pretty much an amicable but wild combat. Hurling was a feature of most village feast days in Cornwall, but the event at St. Columb is a rare survival. So important was it that the parish church contains an image of a hurling ball carved on an ancient bench end.

Like hurling, Cornish 'wrassling' is unique to the county. The Red Lion pub is proud of a former landlord, James Polkinghorne, Cornwall's most famous wrestler. Cornishmen went into battle at Agincourt in 1415 bearing aloft their banner depicting two wrestlers – their principal pastime and at which they excelled. An unusual memorial on the pub wall depicts Polkinghorne in action against Abraham Cann, champion of Devon, for the title of West Country Champion in 1826.

BLISLAND – rock carvings

Location:
four miles north-east of Bodmin

OS map:
200 1036 7437

Sat nav:
PL30 4JT

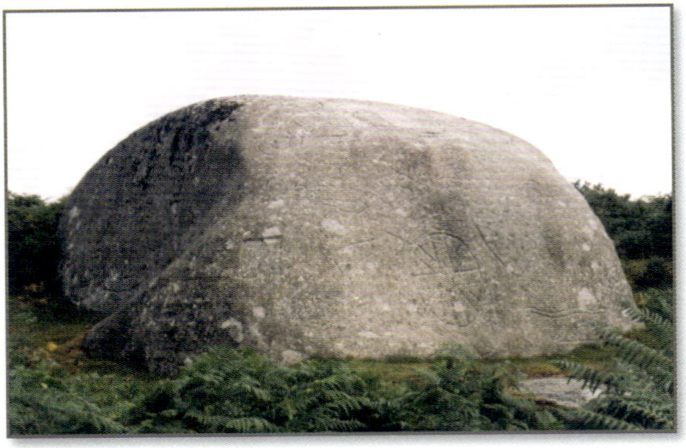

Blisland is a quiet, remote village with the only parish church in England dedicated to the third-century martyrs St. Protus and St. Hyacinth. A mile to the north, 700ft above sea level, is Jubilee Rock. It's even quieter and more remote but worth the walk for the outstanding views you have across the moorland.

In October, 1810, Lieutenant Rogers of the 65th Regiment was sent on a recruiting mission. Being nearby, he called to visit his family at Pendrift, and decided they must somehow commemorate the fiftieth year of the reign of George III. Together with his platoon of soldiers, he carved a figure of Britannia into this great boulder, along with royal and other armorials, those of the Rogers family of Blisland, and various agricultural and industrial symbols.

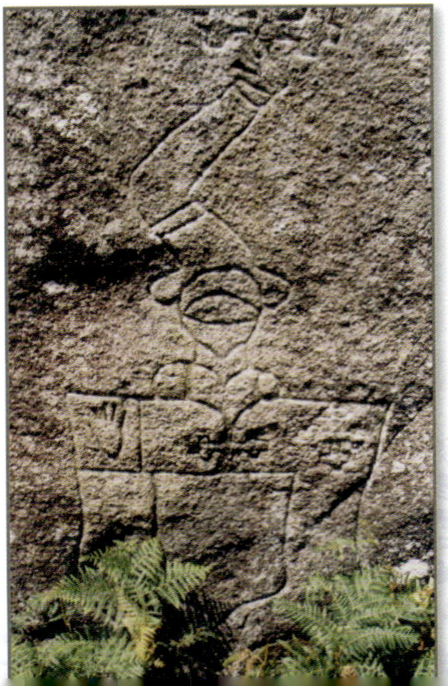

A later, unknown, but equally loyal subject carved the arms of Queen Victoria on the top of the rock in celebration of her Golden Jubilee in 1887.

BODMIN – a dog trough

Location:
in Bodmin's main car park

OS map:
200 0599 6689

Sat nav:
PL31 2DQ

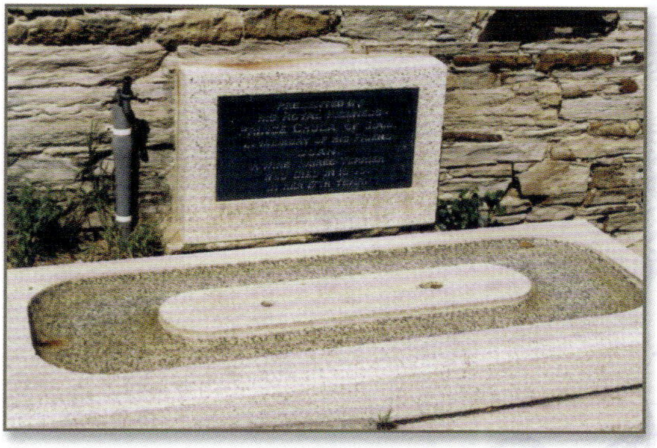

Bodmin is home to many curiosities and historical artefacts, but we have chosen a dog drinking trough because it is so easy to miss – unless your dog is thirsty! You will find it at the entrance to Priory Park, where you can leave your car. It is inscribed:

> *Presented by His Highness Prince Chula Chakrabongse of Siam in memory of his friend Joan, a wire-haired terrier who died in 1948.*
>
> *Further endowed in memory of the bulldog Hercules, 1954*

You may be wondering why a Prince of Siam (now Thailand) wished to endow a dog drinking trough in Bodmin? Like a lot of people, he had fallen in love with all things Cornish. After being educated at Harrow and Cambridge and a short spell in Siam he returned to England. Here he married a local girl, Elizabeth Hunter, and they settled at Tredethy, St. Mabyn.

Amongst other interests, he set up his own motor racing team.With his cousin, Biri, as driver, they had some successes in their particular class of cars at World Championship level, but parted in 1948. The Prince also established Narisa Hall at Bodmin as a centre for music and dancing, and a clinic for mothers and children.

ST. EVAL – RAF memorial

Location:
five miles south of Padstow

OS map:
200 8272 6931

Sat nav:
PL27 7UF

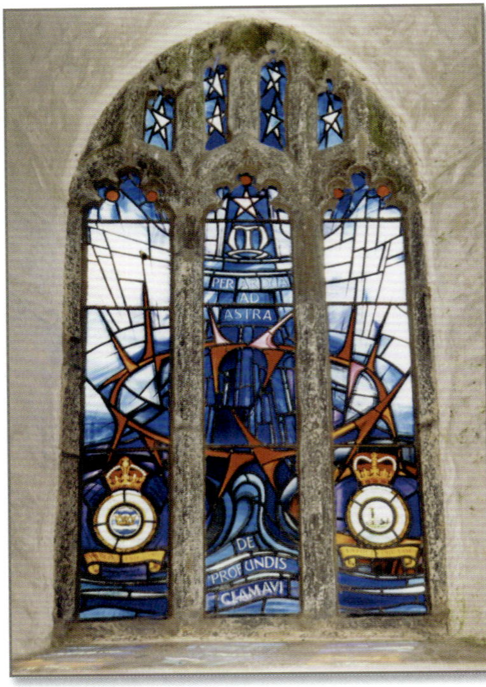

The church of St. Uvelus has been a beacon of Christianity for centuries. It has such a prominent tower that it was used as a daymark by passing vessels. It was considered so important that it was rebuilt by Bristol's merchants between 1724–27. Later, during WW II, those young pilots who taxied out from the now-deserted concrete runways also used the church tower as a beacon for landing and its outline forms part of their badge of Coastal Command.

The east window, designed by Crear McCarthey, is a dramatic memorial to them. The red of the RAF roundel has been transformed into Christ's Crown of Thorns, the circles at the foot symbolise the storm-tossed sea around Cornwall, and the stars of the RAF motto occupy the tracery at the top. It is a response to Psalm 130.

Outside are the headstones of the young airmen from Britain and the Commonwealth who undertook so many the dangerous missions and paid the ultimate price.

ST. MERRYN – a monumental collection

Location:
three miles south-west of Padstow

OS map:
200 8919 7480

Sat nav:
PL28 8JZ

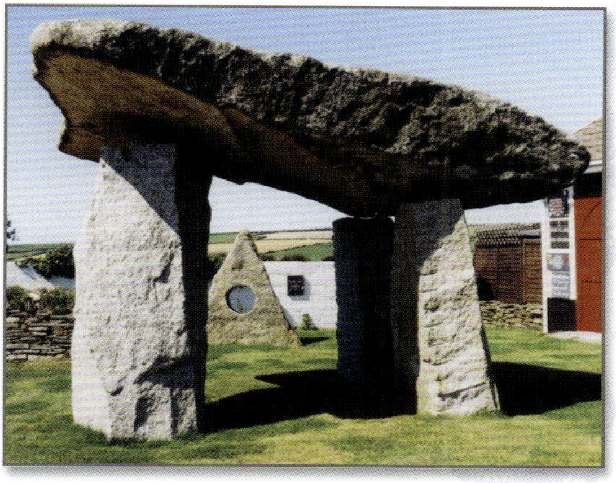

A short distance inland from Trevose Head is a private garden full of huge granite monuments, which the builder believes are charged with mystical power. The first, a ten-ton Rocking (or Logan) Stone, was raised on St. Piran's Day, March 5, 1982, since when the collection has grown. The Seven Sisters are each named after a 'powerful' lady in the builder's life, with their circle's centre stone as Man the Peacemaker – there to tackle any problems the Sisters cannot deal with!

The Healing Stone is a replica of the Men-an-tol stone and is said to have helped many people since it was erected in 1984, especially those with back troubles. Two years later a Wedding Stone was erected and a ceremony devised, with a certificate for anyone who wishes to 'marry' for a year and a day. A massive quoit was brought in 1987 and a fogou added in 1992, a "magic underground chamber" 12ft (3.66m) below ground, which took six months to complete.

You can visit by appointment by contacting the builder and owner, Ed Prynn at the Stones, Tresallyn Cross, St Merryn. Tel 01841 5221045

PADSTOW – founding fathers

Location:
four miles west of
Wadebridge

OS map:
200 9194 7549

Sat nav:
PL28 8AF

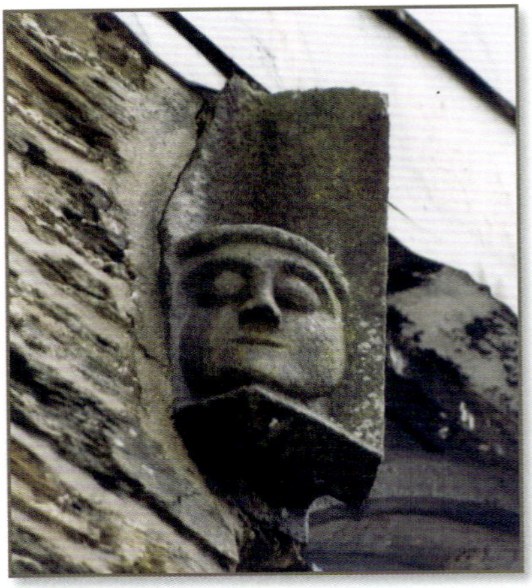

Nineteenth-century guidebooks were not enthusiastic about Padstow: it was "a mean-looking place, of woebegone aspect". But times change. Once the ecclesiastical capital of Cornwall, it was also a great fishing port. In the days when Cornwall's minerals and other products were transported by boat it provided, with Hayle, one of the only two estuaries on the treacherous north coast where vessels could seek shelter.

Much of that vitality and character has been retained although its economy is now based on visitors, who throng on May Day to watch the primeval 'Obby 'Oss unleashed to dance and do battle with the Teazer.

The medieval quayside buildings have changed function too but are intact and relatively unspoiled. On South Quay, the 16th-century Court House is where Sir Walter Raleigh presided as Warden of Cornwall. Even older – possibly one of the oldest houses in Cornwall – the 15th-century Abbey House was Guild House and chapel for Padstow's merchants: was this curious carving a portrait one of those men?

WADEBRIDGE – the wool bridge

Location:
on A39, four miles east of Padstow

OS map:
200 9915 7240

Sat nav:
PL27 7AQ

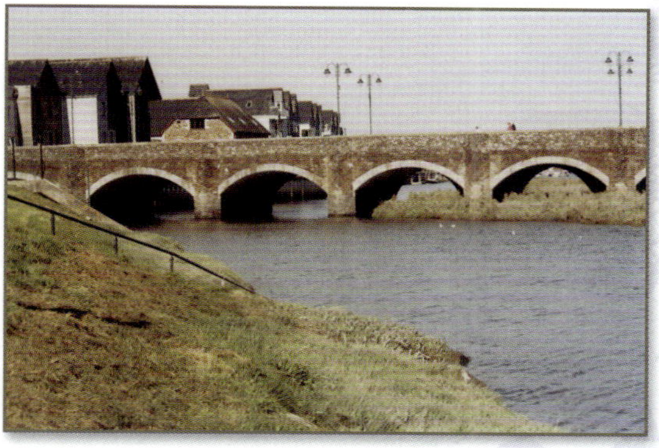

Wadebridge is interesting for several reasons, but especially its bridge. 'Wade' indicates that the Romans had crossed the river Camel at this 'vadum' or ford, which then became the English 'waed'. Later, in the Middle Ages there was so much traffic across that chapels were erected on either side: St. Michael's on the St. Breock bank, licensed in 1382, and King's Chapel opposite, where travellers could pray for a safe crossing or wait for low tide. Sometime about 1468 a bridge was built, 320 ft long.

As a result of the efforts of John Lovibond, vicar of Egloshayle, the money to fund it came mostly from taxes on the profits of the wool trade, which gave rise to the expression 'a bridge built on wool'. Though wool does solidify when compressed wet, in this case the saying is just a figurative reminder of the local source of wealth.

One of the granite coping stones has a hole where parts of the body of a Catholic priest, Cuthbert Mayne, were displayed after he was hung, drawn and quartered in Launceston in 1577. The bridge was chosen as one of the more prominent sites from which to warn others to remain faithful to the new Church of England. Mayne's skull is preserved in the Carmelite monastery at Lanherne (St. Mawgan) and he was canonised by Pope Paul VI in 1970.

ST. ENDELLION – a saint's shrine

Location:
five miles north of Wadebridge

OS map:
200 9968 7874

Sat nav:
PL29 3TP

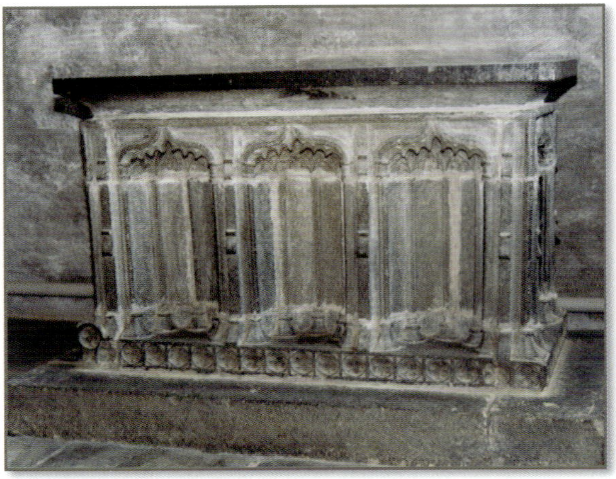

St. Endelienta was the daughter of a 6th-century Welsh king, Brychan. She came from a large family and other villages in the area are named after her sisters: St. Minver, St. Teath and St. Mabyn.

Endelienta lived the austere life of a hermit and her only food was milk from her cow. Unfortunately, the animal strayed onto the land of the local lord, who killed it. He in turn was killed by her godfather, King Arthur. However, all ended well when Endelienta restored both lord and cow back to life.

She had expressed a wish that when she died her body should be put on a cart and wherever the young cattle pulling it stopped, there she would be buried. Her church stands on that spot. She herself is said to be under the carved slate altar tomb which was added 800 years later, a fine example of medieval craftsmanship by the 'Master of St. Endellion'.

PORTQUIN – a party piece

Location:
six miles north of Wadebridge

OS map:
200 9713 8053

Sat nav:
PL29 3SU

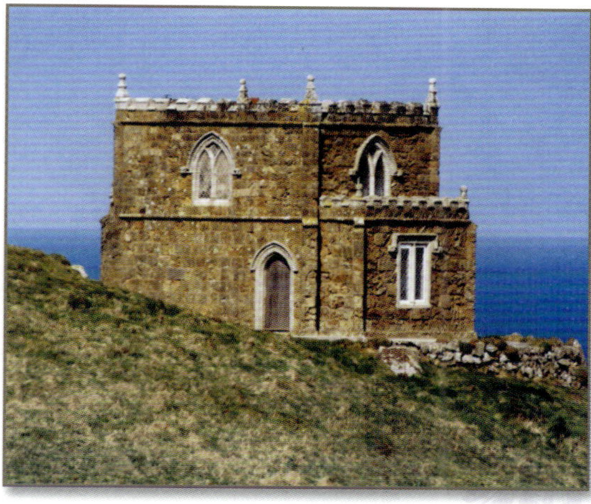

Perched on Doyden Point specifically to capture the stunning views, Doyden Castle is really a 19th-century folly. In 1839 the local bon-viveur Samuel Symons of Gonvena House, Wadebridge, decided to build a place where he could be alone or, alternatively, entertain his friends to nights of dining, drinking and dicing – the sizeable wine bins are evidence of the conviviality of his parties.

Even in those days, drinking and driving was not recommended. Symons always drove his pony and gig from his house round the track on the cliff side (not for the faint hearted) to his castle so that when he was ready to return home the horse could take the safer inland path. More recently, the exterior of Doyden Castle appeared in the popular Poldark television series, as Dr. Dwight Enys's house.

ST. KEW – bell ringers' rules

Location:
three miles north-east of Wadebridge

OS map:
200 0218 7689

Sat nav:
PL30 3EP

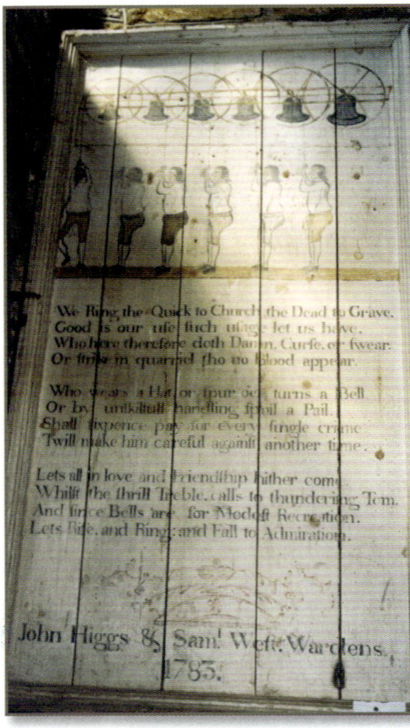

According to legend, St. Kewe built the first church on this very same spot. Centuries later, a panel was hung in the tower, dated 1783 and showing the church's six bells and six ringers, beneath which is a Georgian 'Ringers' Rhyme', a quaint set of rules:

We ring the Quick to Church the Dead to Grave.
Good is our use such usage let us have.
Who here therefore doth Damn, Curse, or Swear.
Or strike in quarriel tho no Blood appear.

Who wears a Hat or Spur oer turns a Bell.
Or by unskilfull handling spoil a Pail.
Shall sixpence pay for every single crime.
Twill make him careful against another time.

Lets all in love and Friendship hither come.
Whilst the shrill Treble calls to thundering Tom.
And since Bells are for Modest Recreation.
Lets Rise and Ring: and Fall to Admiration.

PORT ISAAC – a tight squeeze

Location:
six miles north of Wadebridge

OS map:
200 9964 8083

Sat nav:
PL29 3RB

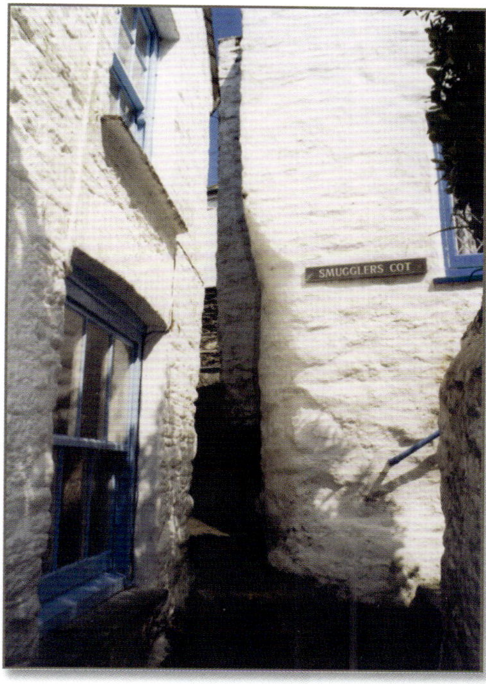

Port Isaac has been a fishing harbour far longer than the home of Doc Martin. Its name often puzzles those unfamiliar with the Cornish language, in which 'porth ysack' means simply 'corn port' – although until the 19th century it also traded in pilchards, stone and slate.

The harbour was the only shelter on this part of the coast and many of the fishermen's cottages hug the steeply-sided bay, creating a network of exceptionally narrow streets and alleyways which tumble down to the small beach.

The main Fore Street is only 7ft (2.1m) wide while the colloquially named Sqeeze-ee-belly Alley is just 19½ inches (495mm) across, the narrowest of these 'drangs', and is included in the *Guinness Book of Records*. Many of the properties are like doll's houses. One, the Bird Cage, now owned by the National Trust, is a tall, asymmetrical building. Originally a fisherman's cottage, it neatly fills the exceedingly narrow space available.

TINTAGEL – monument to miners

Location:
on B3263, five miles north-west of Camelford

OS map:
200 0478 8647

Sat nav:
PL34 0HB

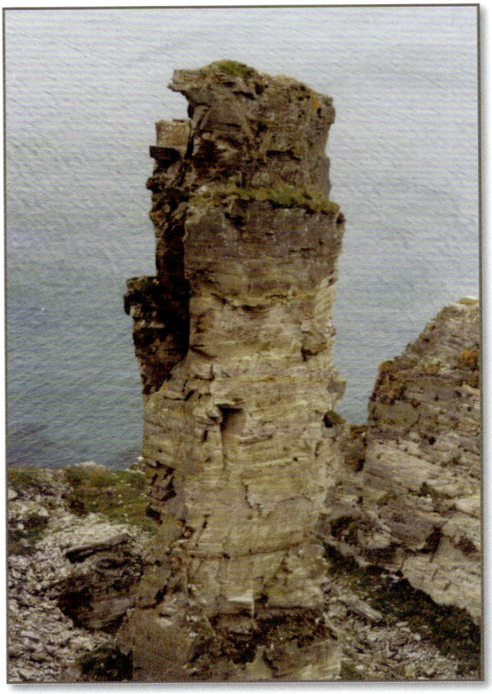

However perplexing the tangle of myth and legend obscuring Tintagel's actual history, there is a lot to interest us here. The rugged, dramatic cliffs were quarried extensively for slate, mainly by men lowered from the top in harness, operated by a donkey 'whim', or standing on wooden staging. The slate itself was then lowered into small boats and delivered to where it was required.

At one quarry, Lanterdan, the workmen left us a reminder of their work: a pinnacle about 80ft (24.4m) high standing on the shore between the cliff-face and the sea.

The industry continues to thrive not far away at Delabole, where the quarry has been worked for over 1,000 years (and has reserves for another 1,000 and more). It is over 1½ miles in circumference and was once the deepest man-made hole in the world. There is also the first commercial wind farm built in the UK.

CAMELFORD – murder– but who did it?

Location:
on A39, ten miles
north of Bodmin

OS map:
200 1378 8162

Sat nav:
PL32 9QG

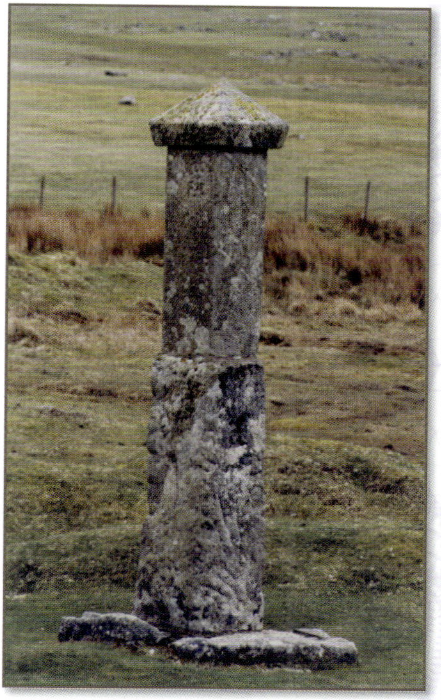

Roughtor is the second highest point of Bodmin Moor. At the bottom is an unusually-shaped granite column inscribed:

IN MEMORY OF
CHARLOTTE DYMOND
MURDERED BY MATTHEW WEEKES
ON SUNDAY, APRIL 14, 1844.

On that fateful day Charlotte, a housemaid at Penhale, went for a walk over the moor with her lover, Matthew Weekes. Only Matthew returned, saying Charlotte had gone on to visit Tom Prout, another farm labourer. Days later a search began and at the same time Weekes disappeared.

Charlotte's body was found and Weekes was traced to Plymouth. His subsequent conviction and hanging at Bodmin relied entirely on circumstantial evidence, leaving the true course of events something of a mystery about which there is still considerable debate. Charlotte was buried in Davidstowe churchyard, her grave unmarked on the insistence of the vicar so not to attract unwelcome attention.

ROCKY VALLEY – mosses and mazes

Location:
off B3263, one mile north of Bossiney

OS map:
200 0723 8939

Sat nav:
PL34 0BB

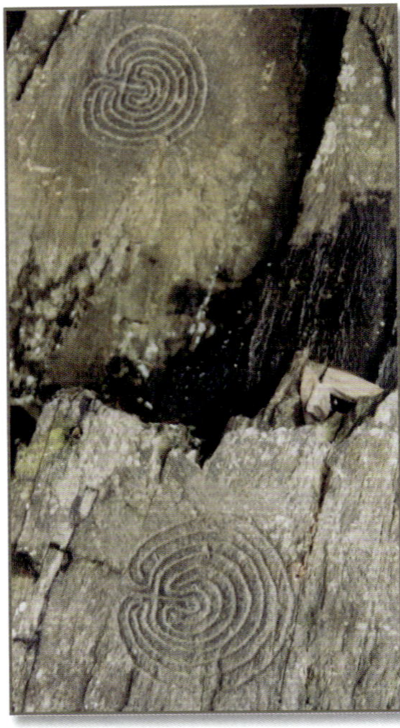

Rocky Valley is nationally important as 161 different species of mosses have been recorded here. There are carvings too: two labyrinth patterns incised into the rock on the eastern bank of the stream.

No-one is quite certain where or when labyrinth patterns started or what they were for. Some say they were inspired by the legend of the monstrous Minotaur while others that they are a symbol of death, or map of the Underworld, a path of penance, or a venue for a springtime fertility rite.

The Minotaur was a mythical beast – half man, half bull that lived in the Cretan Labyrinth and devoured young maidens and youths. The Greek hero Theseus slew him.

Opinion is similarly divided about the origin of these particular carvings in Rocky Valley. They may date from the Bronze Age but they seem to have been cut by a metal tool and are well-preserved, so are probably Celtic. But as the rock face was cut back in connection with the ruined watermill nearby, were they carved by the miller a couple of hundred years ago? Why? And how did he know about such designs?

SLAUGHTERBRIDGE – Arthur's grave?

Location:
one mile north of Camelford

OS map:
200 1111 8562

Sat nav:
PL32 9XQ

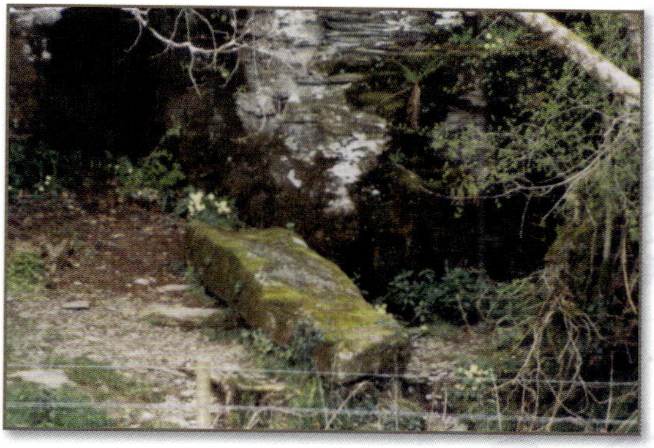

Only a short distance from Tintagel, in AD 539 or 542 (depending on which book you read), King Arthur is said to have led his Celtic forces in his last battle. Here, where the lane crosses the river Camel, according to a twelfth-century priest,

> *...gathered sixty thousand and more. Mordred was their leader. And the noble Arthur rode there with a huge army, although it was doomed. On the river Camel they fought together, sparks flew out, spurs shattered, shields broke, shafts snapped, the mighty host fought together there the Camel was in flood with measureless blood.*

Mordred was killed and Arthur mortally wounded.

Now covered with moss and embedded in the river bank is a large granite slab inscribed in both ogham (an ancient Celtic script, which dates the stone to around the 6th century) and Latin:

> *Latini* [h]*ic iacet fili Ma*[..]*ri – Latini son of Macari lies here.*

Some however think the last word is really "Magni Arturi", Arthur the Great. If this is so, it may be a memorial to that last battle. Sadly, though, for those of us of a romantic nature the strength of evidence is that it is connected to a later Celtic chieftain. Yet in popular mythology this is Arthur's grave and always will be. Such is his magical power.

STRATTON – a civil war...

Location:
twenty miles north of Launceston

OS map:
190 2264 0714

Sat nav:
arch EX23 9EY
inn EX23 9DA

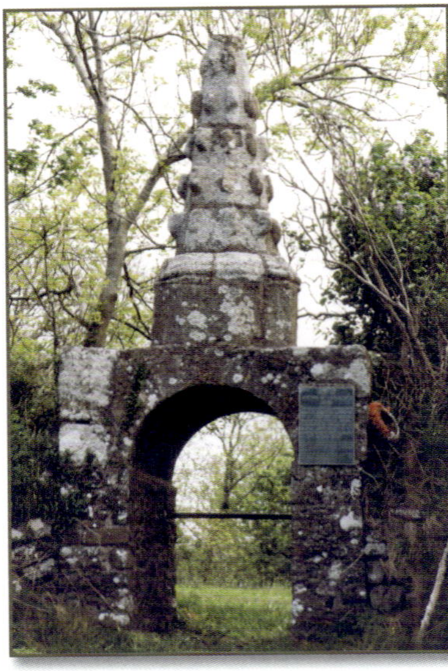

Though principally supportive of the King during the English Civil Wars, Cornwall was typical of a nation 'by the sword divided' – family against family. One of the early significant battles took place near Stratton. On 16 May 1643, 6,000 Parliamentarians arrived and made a stand. At the head of the Royalists were Sir Ralph Hopton and Sir Bevil Grenville. Grenville was from a family steeped in military history, dear to the Cornish, and was defending his home patch.

The Royalists knew they were outnumbered and outgunned but spurred on by their leaders attacked with great courage and determination. The battle raged all day, until towards the evening Sir Bevil was:

> *borne to the ground but quickly relieved by his companion Sir John Barkeley they re-enforced the charge and won the day.*

Three hundred soldiers were killed and 1,700 taken prisoner.

The battlefield at Stamford Hill is marked by a small arch, crowned with a crocketed pinnacle which originally stood on Poughill church tower.

...and a giant

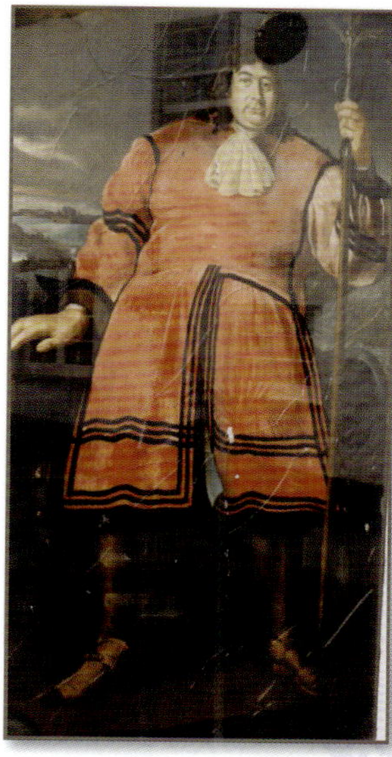

The old plaque is on the side of the Tree Inn and reads:

in this place ye Army of ye Rebels under ye command of ye
Earl of Stamford received A signal overthrow by ye valour of
S Bevill Grenville and ye Cornish army on Tuesday May 16 1643.

Inside the inn are scythes said to have been used in the battle, and in the courtyard is a full-length portrait of local hero Anthony Payne, who was born and died at the manor house, now the Tree Inn. Known as the 'Cornish Giant', 7ft 4ins (2.24m) tall and weighing 38 stones (241k), this huge man devoted his whole life to the service of Sir Bevil, fighting with him at Stamford Hill and bringing home his body when he was killed at Lansdown, near Bath on July 5, 1643. He is shown in a painting of 1680 wearing his uniform of Halbadier of the guns of Plymouth Citadel.

There are many stories about him. When he died, the only way his coffin could be brought downstairs was through a hole made in the floor. Then there is a reference to his sword in the rhyme:

His sword was made to match his size,
As Roundheads did remember;
And when it swung 'twas like the whirl
Of windmills in September.

MORWENSTOW – an eccentric parson

Location:
six miles north of Bude

OS map:
190 2058 1539

Sat nav:
EX23 9SR

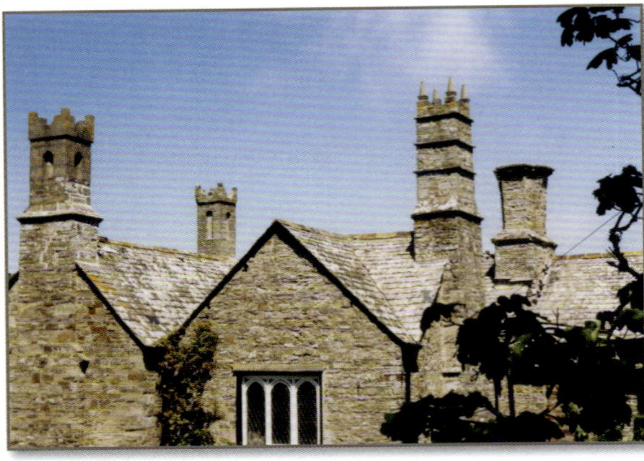

In the remote, far northern tip of Cornwall, the tower of the church of SS Morwenna and John has for centuries been a landmark for passing ships, but it is also famous for a former incumbent, the Revd. Robert Stephen Hawker.

Parson Hawker was a genuine original, a mystic, natural wit and poet with a vibrant and eccentric personality. He arrived in this windswept parish in 1834 at the age of 31 and spent the next 41 years serving "a mixed multitude of smugglers, wreckers and dissenters." He delighted in attracting attention and left his mark in many ways.

The vicarage was in ruins when he arrived so he built a new one in Victorian Gothic style, copying it from Thomas Hunt's book of 1827, *Designs for Parsonage Houses*. Idiosyncratically, he modelled five of its chimney-stacks on the towers of churches where he had served earlier – Stratton, Whitstone, and North Tamarton, and two Oxford colleges – while the kitchen chimney was styled on his mother's tomb.